I LIVE WITH ADHD

WRITTEN BY CHRISTINA EARLEY

ILLUSTRATED BY
AMANDA HUDSON

A Starfish Book

SEAHORSE
PUBLISHING

Teaching Tips for Caregivers:

As a caregiver, you can help your child succeed in school by giving them a strong foundation in language and literacy skills and a desire to learn to read.

This book helps children grow by letting them practice reading skills.

Reading for pleasure and interest will help your child to develop reading skills and will give your child the opportunity to practice these skills in meaningful ways.

- Encourage your child to read on her own at home
- Encourage your child to practice reading aloud
- Encourage activities that require reading
- Establish a reading time
- Talk with your child
- Give your child writing materials

Teaching Tips for Teachers:

Research shows that one of the best ways for students to learn a new topic is to read about it.

Before Reading

- Read the "Words to Know" and discuss the meaning of each word.
- Read the back cover to see what the book is about.

During Reading

- When a student gets to a word that is unknown, ask them to look at the rest of the sentence to find clues to help with the meaning of the unknown word.
- Ask the student to write down any pages of the book that were confusing to them.

After Reading

- Discuss the main idea of the book.
- Ask students to give one detail that they learned in the book by showing a text dependent answer from the book.

TABLE OF CONTENTS

I Live with ADHD

Hi! My name is Finn.

I am nine years old.

I live with my mom and sister Sadie.
Steve and Harvey are my guinea pigs.

I was born with ADHD. That means *attention deficit hyperactivity disorder*.

I have a hard time remembering things.
My body likes to keep moving.

ADHD is a brain **disorder**. Some people with the disorder have problems paying attention.

Others have high energy and are **impulsive**. Many have a combination.

I ride the bus to school. My friend Manny sits next to me.

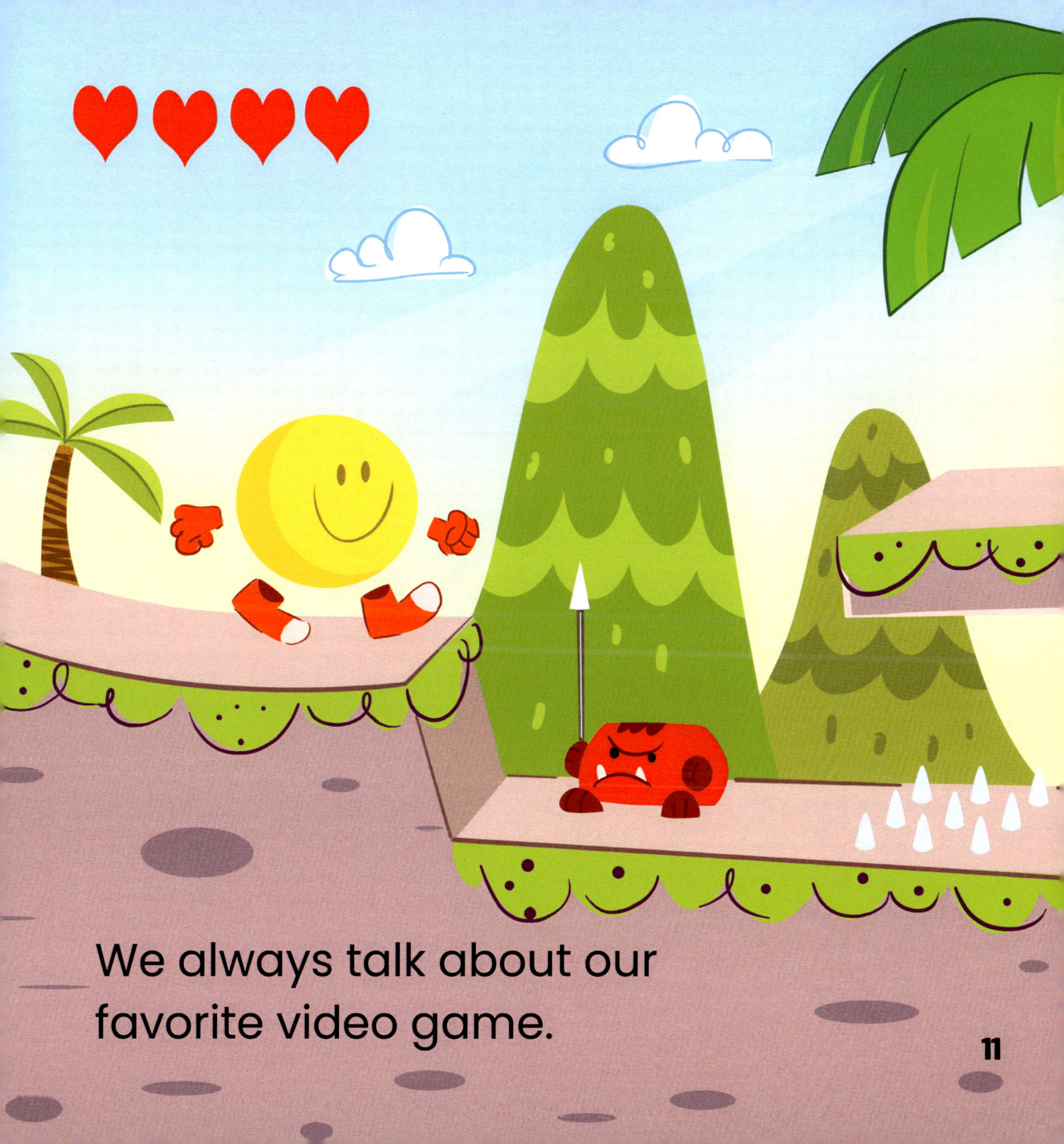

We always talk about our
favorite video game.

I have a chart on my desk. It helps me remember what I need to do.

I work with Mr. Bell on my reading. I have a bookmark with **strategies**.

Mindfulness **meditation** trains my brain to focus. I do this before I do my homework.

I play soccer on the Princeton Turtles soccer team. I run with the ball at lightning speed!

I like to write **original** songs. I make goofy videos, too.

When I grow up, I want to have my own television show. What do you want to do when you grow up?

LEARN ABOUT ADHD

What Is ADHD?

ADHD stands for *attention deficit hyperactivity disorder*. It is a lifelong medical condition of the brain that affects attention and self-control. People with ADHD can be easily distracted, hyperactive, and impulsive. This makes learning at school challenging.

Those with ADHD also have strengths. Some have hyperfocus, or the ability to focus on a task for hours. Many show resilience as they find ways to overcome obstacles. People with ADHD are often highly creative and can think of unusual solutions from a unique perspective.

Scientists are not sure what causes the brain differences of ADHD. It is believed to be inherited. Many children who have ADHD also have a parent or relative who has it, too. It is not caused by having too much screen time, poor parenting, or eating too much sugar.

Some people choose to treat ADHD with medicine. Behavior therapy helps children learn how to be less disruptive to others. Teachers can provide support with organizational skills and strategies to help with remembering tasks. With the right supports, children with ADHD grow into adults who can manage their condition and have successful relationships and careers.

Websites to Visit

ADDitude: additudemag.com

ADHD Aware: adhdaware.org

Attention Deficit Disorder Organization: add.org

Children and Adults with Attention-Deficit/Hyperactivity Disorder: chadd.org

Totally ADD: totallyadd.com

Take the Pledge for Inclusion

- ☑ I accept people of all abilities.
- ☑ I respect others and act with kindness and compassion.
- ☑ I include people with special needs and disabilities in my school and in my community.

Get your parent's permission to sign the online pledge at PledgeforInclusion.org.

Famous People with ADHD

Simone Biles: Olympic gymnast

Walt Disney: Creator of Mickey Mouse

Michael Jordan: NBA player

Michael Phelps: Olympic swimmer

Dav Pilkey: Author of *Captain Underpants* books

Justin Timberlake: Entertainer

Simone Biles

Michael Jordan

Celebrate and Educate

ADHD Awareness Month happens in October.

Inclusive Schools Week is the first full week in December.

WORDS TO KNOW

disorder (dis-OR-dur): a physical or mental condition that is unusual

impulsive (im-PUHL-siv): acting without thinking

meditation (med-i-TAY-shuhn): the act of thinking deeply and quietly

original (uh-RIJ-uh-nuhl): new, interesting, and not copied from something else; the first of a kind

strategies (STRAT-i-jeez): specific plans or methods for reaching a goal

INDEX

COMPREHENSION QUESTIONS

1. ADHD stands for ___.

   a. attention deficit hyperactivity disorder

   b. all day happy day

   c. always do homework

2. The Princeton Turtles is a _____ team.

   a. cheerleading

   b. basketball

   c. soccer

3. The names of Finn's guinea pigs are ____.

   a. Salt and Pepper

   b. Steve and Harvey

   c. Mick and Mike

4. True or False: Finn has a hard time remembering things.

5. True or False: A person only has ADHD as a child.

Answers: 1. a, 2. c, 3. b, 4. True, 5. False

ABOUT THE AUTHOR

Christina Earley lives in sunny south Florida with her son, husband, and rescue dog. She has been teaching children with special needs for over 25 years. She loves to bake cookies, read books about animals, and ride roller coasters.

Written by: Christina Earley
Illustrated by: Amanda Hudson
Design by: Under the Oaks Media
Editor: Kim Thompson

Photos: A.RICARDO//Shutterstock: p. 21 (Simone Biles); landmarkmedia/Shutterstock: p. 21 (Michael Jordan)

Library of Congress PCN Data
I Live with ADHD /Christina Earley
I Live With
ISBN 979-8-8873-5343-2(hard cover)
ISBN 979-8-8873-5428-6(paperback)
ISBN 979-8-8873-5513-9(EPUB)
ISBN 979-8-8873-5598-6(eBook)
Library of Congress Control Number: 2022948906

Printed in Canada/202312/CP20231201

Seahorse Publishing Company
www.seahorsepub.com

Published in the United States
Seahorse Publishing
PO Box 771325
Coral Springs, FL 33077